MW01127423

The Red Desk

Mary Kim Schreck

Published by Tigress Press, LLC
Columbia, Missouri

ISBN 0-9771601-0-6

Published July 2005

Published in the United States of America
Tigress Press, LLC
P O Box 30859
Columbia, MO 65205-3859
www.tigresspress.com

Dedication

For my husband, Bernard Schreck, who "walked his talk" and profoundly influenced everyone he contacted with his wisdom and vision – truly the educational leader.

Contents

THE RED DESK

The Red Desk

Amulet, totem, symbol –
my red desk,
easily over seventy-five years old now.

Deep initials and names cover its surface.
Carved by bored boys in detentions,
or in seemingly endless study halls –
carved before pocketknives
were banned from jeans' pockets –
in the old days.

I rescued the desk
before its mates were sent to the warehouse,
before newer flimsier fare
took their places.

I dragged that heavy hunk of iron and wood
to my classroom.
And with cans of apple red spray paint
transformed it into a
gleaming jewel.

Twenty plus years that red desk
housed treasures under its lid,
housed me in front of my classes.

In fall
it was the teacher's desk
cozied up to the class – breaking
the tension that the formal desk behind
me necessitated.

In winter
it was where I conferenced
young writers who nudged a small stool
up to its broad desk top
to share the writing, the whispering,
the space with me.

In spring
it was the Poet's Chair
where students sat and directed
the class's attention to the reading
of their poems.

It was with sacred melancholy
later
that a couple students carried it out to our pickup –
my last day of school.
Now it resides
in a sweet little room
with a view of the lake and gardens
still filled with treasures
still the amulet, totem, symbol
of my life's most joyous preoccupation –
teaching.

Morning Announcements

Attention Teachers:
There is no magic bullet!
You are
the magic
you are
the power, the strength
of the bullet
sent out to strike chords
and change forever
young minds.

Teachers:
Let go
of your hope
that some time, somewhere –
if only
you go to enough workshops,
read enough journals,
collect enough lessons –
you'll find
the right answer.

Teachers:
You are the answer.
You are
the silver bullet.

Embrace
the beauty, the power
that is your legacy...
Relax,
enjoy, go within –
dip into your own private well
for meaning –
then teach!

The First Day of School

I am again the little girl
with fat braids
in my blue uniform and new shoes
with new school supplies.

Leaving for school
hoping the bullies won't be so bad
hoping the teachers will like me.

I'm still the little girl
with heart clutched by anticipation
excitement
a slim thread of dread
and a big dose of vulnerability.

I'm the little girl
who is now the teacher.

Teaching Literature in A Material Culture

How do you convince
today's teenagers
that reading, learning,
becoming filled up with new thought
is a good in itself?

How do you stand up –
so tiny a figure in a dense crowd
and disagree with the notion
that money making is the sole
purpose of life?

Sadly, the spirit
that needs wings of disciplined thought
and quiet
(God forbid, quiet)
to soar up and out of its flesh
is caged all too often.

The drums
of greed, ownership, accumulation
beat down the spirit
and twist one's purpose
into strange unnatural shapes.

Yet,
we touch – in those precious moments
when the world stays outside our doors
and the beauty and power
of the words we read
take on a shimmering life of their own –
we touch
young minds
with the notion that yes, indeed,
there exists another realm

of existence
that they too can reach...
and perhaps
find deeply satisfying
and worth
the journey of pursuit.

For these moments
these rarified moments
we teachers live.

Pleasant Dreams

I dreamed
the blue morning glories
detached
from their vines
and flew away
as beautiful butterflies...
I was delighted.

A Field Trip

Students:
Today we will be visiting a glasses maker.
Not the kind that fix problems
originating in your eyes,
but rather near-sightedness of the mind
and cataracts of the heart.

Students.
You will meet Mr. Insight –
a gentle man surrounded by shelves
and shelves filled with glittering glasses
in frames all shapes and sizes.
Notice each shelf carries a different label.
One is marked "avoiding bias"
another "erasing ethnic prejudice"
and still another "seeing past poverty"
and so on and so on.

Now students:
You are free to try on any of the glasses
you wish.
If you can't reach a shelf, just let me know,
I'm here to help you.
Please remember to take notes
on the new clarity each lense affords you
so we can share our findings
when we get back to class.

Yes, Emily, some glasses will be
available for sale at a later date.
Don't forget to take a copy of the brochure
home with you
to share with your parents.

Notice how some glasses make no difference
whatsoever in your current vision
since your eyes might already be open
to the particular view they offer.
When this occurs
please place a star on your sheet.

"Tolerance of differences"
seems to carry the strongest lenses
in the collection.
Be sure to try on and test a pair
by looking at your fellow classmates
and comparing your view of them
before and after.

Are there any questions?
Jason?
Why don't more people know
about this shop? And if they do,
why don't they get a few pairs
so they can see better?

Well, Jason,
many do know but feel they will look funny
if they wore them...
many don't want to risk being different
(that old peer pressure thing)...
others just hate the idea of change
while others can't afford
what changes those glasses
would demand
in how they see and treat others.
Some are just
plain afraid.

Julia? Yes,
if more students were made aware
of these glasses earlier
while they're still young,
that would make it easier to get used
to them.

That's the purpose
of this field trip.
It's my job to help you see better.

Now, let's enjoy the day!

Flock Of Pigeons

As a child
I always wanted a carrier pigeon –
the perfect pet –
useful, exotic, a true conversation piece!

I saw myself
folding tiny messages
attaching them
to red-clawed pigeon feet
then opening the bedroom window
(always a second-story bedroom window
in my imagination)
and releasing my pigeon
into the clouds.

The thrill of release was only equaled
by the thrill of return.
In a flurry of feathers
my pigeon would land on the ledge
and peck at the window
seeking reward
for a trip completed.

Now
my poems are my pigeons
and I release them into the clouds
with just the same thrill
and anticipation.
I send them out
to friendly readers, to strangers
over the internet
through the literary magazines
into the post office –
seeking
souls that resonate.

Strange realities ours –
words as feathers,
folded experiences
attached to clawed, inked feet...
winged wonders
seeking readers...
Returning.

A Mother's Plea

Scary introduction
into the sometimes cruel
ways of the world...
that first bully.

Mean, hurtful words
force little minds
to question
everything we parents
said about them for years.

Is it true, Mommy,
am I fat? Do I have ugly clothes?
Funny hair? Is something wrong with me
because I can't throw a ball?
Because I wear glasses?
What makes those kids laugh at me?

How vulnerable
our funny little selves are –
while we're growing
trying to make sense of things –
to those laughing jokes slung mercilessly
our way.

Bullies
don't have to use force
to do damage – words leave scars
far more potent
than bruised arms, knees, legs.

How do we help our children
to ignore
to protect themselves?

Teachers:
We need you...
we need you to defend
our little ones
to buffer the hateful blows.
We need you
to love our little ones
in spite of their flaws,
their inability to fit in gracefully.

Please
champion our little ones
when we can't be there...
Please.

Books

Worlds folded under flaps
square pound of flesh and life
silent holders of screams
both of delight and pain.

Silent thought of great thinkers
rambling thought of lost souls
humming electric emotions blasting
through paper.

Solace, retreat, escape, glaring truth
all wrapped in glossy covers
sleeping for now
on shelves.

My obsession —
the substance of an unsubstantial
gossamer taste of the world.
Books.

The Address Book

Penciled-in numbers, crossed-out addresses,
the wandering history
of a person's movements
from home to home, from phone to phone.

Names and numbers
unused for years now...
Would they answer today?
Where would the conversation begin?

Names changed
new relationships attached
to the old familiar ones...

Some pages filled to overflowing
to back sheets –
Lots of family in the S's, in the T's...
A world of contact, possible touching
"Keep in Touch"
call, write, touch my life

A little book
holding the webwork of our dealings –
the babysitters (although the children are now
old enough to have their own)
the doctors (some dead now)
some so removed from us
we forget the smell of their waiting rooms.

Lists of cell phones, dorm phones, apartment phones –
the time line of college years
wrapped carefully along a phone line.

More telling than most diaries
more subtle perhaps
the lacquered duck address/phone book
keeps in touch long after we have stopped
reaching out.

A Poem A Day

A poem a day –
or so I would say to myself –
just set pen to paper
and it will write itself
(or so I was taught).

So what will it be?
About curdled time waiting for a call?
About riding the heat bubbles on asphalt
in July's afternoon shower?
About courting my new house
into an easy understanding?

Maybe dig up the planted fears
that bloom and blossom in the dark
around two a.m. when they're my
sole companions...

Maybe probe the relativity of time –
its quick-paced way of measuring out
my months and years –
so fast like the electric meter runs outside
when the heat plays a frantic game of tag
with the air-conditioner –
so fast, so fast.

Maybe
I'll wait tor the right set of words
to tickle my imagination, my emotion
to force me to the page –

Am I but
a pitcher of words
ready to spill upon the page?
Or
a well of words
deep, cool, waiting to be
bucketed up?
A poem a day should tell...should tell...will tell...

A Student Reflects on 'The Gradebook'

Tiny blue boxes in a row
filled with numbers, checks, dots, circles.

And what do they signify?
A journey across the page of efforts?
A map of attempts to communicate?
Or is it more often... "Replicate"
another's opinions or attitudes:
"Did I say what you want me to say?"

Letters and numbers
that doom or display my future relationships...
with art, writing, speaking, risk taking
I do well: I continue with resolve –
if I fall short, stumble: I want to quit,
get the humiliation over.
"No talent in that area," I am told.

How clearly does this mirror reflect
my inner fire?
Does this Red Book filled to the corners
with tiny judges
pronounce judgment over my intelligence
accurately?

And in that grade book mirror
do I like who I see?
Do I have enough trust in the row of numbers
to believe what I see?

Could I be looking instead into a circus mirror
that contorts my mind's size?
Shrinking my abilities
or worse yet,
magnifying my achievements
to laughable proportions?

Somewhere in the maze of scores
I exist.

At times the scores speak of my ingenuity, creativity,
intelligent ability
to ignite genuine insights into meaning...
but mostly they
speak of my perseverance –
my dogged consistency in turning in work on time...
work that only numbs the spirit and anesthetizes the brain.
"Numbed numbers on your page, teacher!"

There's something about a row of grades
that isn't honest.
That makes me leery of taking chances and
perhaps falling, failing to be perfect.
That tries to squeeze the effervescent self
into the confines of a blue box.

Beware of the mocking grin
of the grade book.
It's seldom pure
often a distortion
and dangerous
to the soul...
both of ours.

A Post Middle-Age Love Poem

I get his popcorn
when he's in bed – evenings.
I get his coffee
when he's in bed – mornings.

We love the late afternoons
and while he tends the meat in the Weber,
we watch the live things, the lake, the sunset –
we talk.

Later
he builds the most beautiful fires –
feeds them from early fall to late spring
with wood he's chopped, gathered, stacked.

And with only that fire to light us
we sometimes listen –
he with beer, I with wine –
to our favorite music.
Letting the melodies dance
to the rhythms set by the flames.

I'm not the same passionate lover
of years past
and sometimes I know he misses
the magic of that heat –

But like the glowing coals
that produce the flames in our fireplace now
ours is a steady, mellowed burning love
that saturates our every breath
and warms our words with an intensity
the young can only hope for.

Audience

Who are you?
How do I begin to reach you,
touch you with my handiwork?

You walk in smiling
nicely dressed, accessorized...
a world of experience and opinion
tucked under your glance –

What have I to offer you?
How can I begin to judge
which poem to present,
to pick, that will be the perfect
choice?

What life lines do we share?
Teachers, mothers, wives, sisters –
confident, bold or vulnerable, timid...
Can we meet halfway?

Can we hold hands
within the hypnotic rhythm
of a poem's lines
and find a common chord?

Will the private words
going public –
seeking out a like-minded
listener
find a home in you?

The whole reason
for it all – the writing, the publishing –
is to find you
and hopefully
cover and crowd your mind
with vivid words
that touch you.

Awakening

I woke up.
The dorm was clean and silent,
dead quiet.
I slid from between sheets,
walked barefoot
across cold tile –
the cold linoleum under my feet
was real.

I walked
to a window with the shade popping softly
in and out with the breeze
pressed my cheek against the mesh,
smelled the breeze.
Smelled the overnight smoldering
of burned leaves.
It was fall.

I looked
out the window
saw the country side for the first time;
saw a gangly mongrel sniffing squirrel holes;
saw the black, weaving necklace
of geese cross the moon.

I woke up.

(a FOUND POEM from Once Flew Over the Cuckoo's Nest p. 141-142)

Calendars

Dear Pope Gregory
what have you started?
By mapping out time
into square boxes –
so many to a page,
so many pages to a year –
You have tattooed
our minds
with the notion
that time can be tamed,
can be contained,
humanly handled.
By jotting down
commitments
on a numbered block
of calendar space,
we define our future
bridle in our actions
focus our attention.

All is but
a mental wish,
a fogged over desire
until it reaches
the confines of a calendar.

Then
life is real
actions are bent
around the perimeters
of penciled-in events.

In fact
whole days
are distilled into
the concentrated liquid
of a single hour:
the doctor's appointment,
the practice, the meeting, the visit,
the workshop.
All else, preparation or debriefing
with daily chores
tucked in around the edges.

I've kept small pocket
Hallmark calendars
(free to customers in late fall)
for over thirty five years.
Kept them
in a cherry wood box.
Records of those distilled events
that mark
my path upon this planet –
births, purchases, milestones,
moves, visits, vacations,
relationships begun or ended,
deaths.

Yet,
wasn't life really happening
on those squares
unmarked, still white and empty?
Isn't the fiber of life
the distance between events
rather than
those events themselves?

But
calendars
provide us with ladders
to climb from month to month
with hooks
to hang our dazzle upon
in between our
quieter days.

Days
with blank spaces
filled with secrets,
unwritten anguish
we are reticent to label...

We are oh, so much more
than our calendared activities.
Pope Gregory, what have you done?

Call of the Wild

"...a dog could break its heart through being denied the work that killed it...dogs too old for the toil, or injured, had died because they had been cut out of the traces..." Jack London's Call of the Wild

We old dogs
know joy when we feel it
know the bone-tingling, saturating joy
of doing what we love, over and over.

We old dogs
know the secret of "hard work"
it isn't hard, it isn't work
not if it's the love substance
of our very souls...

We old dogs
paint until the trembling hand
can't hold the brush...
compose even when the ear no longer
hears the beauty of the notes.

We old dogs
teach even when
our classroom doors are closed to us –
our students, dismissed –
we roam the state in search
of momentary classrooms.

We old dogs
give one more final tour
with our aging band of musicians –
we star in one last film
when a prime part requires
an old palsied actress.

We know the delicious taste
of the stage –
the warm bath
of the spotlights...

Although the price in energy
will shorten our very existence,
we sign ourselves up anyway –
another competition
another conference presentation
one final book of poetry.

We old dogs
know what's good for us –
not rest, not retreat
but rather
the precious chance
to toil in the traces
once again.

Chinese Art

At the Saint Louis Art Museum
we gaze at old parchment paintings
with their overpowering natural scenes
dwarfing the tiny house or bridge
or other signs of human occupation.

It looks so far away –
so very foreign – as I gaze and follow
fine brush strokes
forming limbs and leaves,
mountains or valleys
with oddly tinted shades of browns, yellows.

A place I've never been to, not even in my dreams
 – this Chinese landscape –
Then another day,
opening the one-hour photo package,
I am struck by a strange familiarity.
Unknowingly on celluloid
I ,too, have captured a Chinese painting!

My Mid-Missouri hillside in early April...
I stare in disbelief
at the same colors,
same fine brush strokes of Nature,
tiny signs of human occupation.

My camera –
made in China – must have known home
when it clicked its shudder.

Confessions of A Happy Teacher

I confess
nothing is so satisfying
as watching
the lessons I've worked so hard
to create
play out better
than could have been imagined.

Nothing can compare
with the feeling
of having taught well:
watching eyes light up
curiosity ignited
smiles on student faces.

I apologize
but I'm happy with my schedule
my number of students
my current grade level.

I actually
love coming to school.
Yes, often I arrive early –
and yes, I find teaching fun.

Of course
I have my bad days –
who doesn't?
But they don't spread
a layer of poison
over me and
they don't infect others.

Yes,
I'm guilty
of spending more time
than many on my preparations –
spending way too much money
on supplies –
but I'm addicted to the joy
of teaching well
and can't help myself.

I admit to stealing.
Stealing every "cool idea,"
strategy, lesson
I can.
No new teaching idea is safe
while I'm around.
Call me an academic klepto
if you wish.

And while I'm at it –
I might as well admit
that I worry.
I have a hard time
forgetting about my students
when that last bell rings.

I want them safe
and happy and loved
when they leave my room.
I want life
to be as fair to them
As I try to be.

Judge me
however you may.
I confess
that "teacher"
is the most beautiful title
I could ever possess
and my proudest
descriptor to date.

Creative Nomad

New toy –
size of a deck of cards
with a long umbilical cord
attached to my ear.

Push the button
and I am electronically connected
to the pulsing underbelly
of the universe –

Waves of sound
(personally, logically selected)
now burst
into emotional, vibrating
blossom.

Oh – slippery, slidy slope
tingling with such a rush –
(brakes, where are they located?)

I must nibble carefully
at this juiced up emotional fruit –
rein in the fire storm it starts
don't give it too much oxygen
keep the stream thin, manageable...

That raging hungry beast within –
must keep him sedated,
rumbling in his dreams...
Don't feed him too much fresh meat
Don't awaken his taste
for more hardy sustenance
than dreams can provide –

Too much feeling in music, be careful!

Where is the warning label
on my new toy?
(this pied piper's instrument
carrying the siren's song)
yet would I heed its warning
if there were one?

With a push of a button
I gingerly step
into a world electric
with life –
raw, untamed,
utterly authentic.

Deep Sea Fishing

King fish, groupers, sailfish,
barracuda, dolphin, tarpon...
a world teeming with life
below the surface.
Variation, variegated...
just below the shifting surface.

We let out line go
watch the spool spin down
wonder what will see the bait
will grab – with quicksilver speed –
the bait.
Our control over the catch
so limited, so left to fate.

And what of our life catches?
Career, mate, children, neighbors, schools –
deep sea trolling life's waters
sometimes we snag a trophy,
sometimes not.

Early Signs

A tiny stand of daffodils
shakes yellow heads
in the breeze.

Nothing else
seems to have changed –
everything else is
stuck in a solid winter mode.

But those
brave little golden ruffles
atop bright green stems
mark our memory
with what might be coming –

Early signs –
subtle alerts of possible change
knock at our subconscious
rock our minds gently
with the rhythms of something
new
just over the horizon.

And we become aware...

Many early signs
are not sweet as daffodils –
some are subtle changes
in our bodies
heralding problems we
would rather ignore.

The first touch
of something hard
beneath the skin...
or sight of
something new and dark and hard
upon the skin...

Those slight lapses
in relationships
that left unattended
lead to chasms, to irreparable
separations.

The shift in conversation,
in body language resisting for now
the effort to wrap with words
what change surely exists...

Some early signs
dribble from our minds –
forgetfulness, confusion,
a drifting feeling
alerting us perhaps
to a future
of virtual shut down and loss.

Early signs – all –
but now
I prefer the daffodils –
Ah, spring will be here soon.

Easter

I know Resurrection –
the sweet taste of "one more time"
the affiliation once more
with a school, with passing bells...

Wearing the name badge
bejeweled with accumulated pins
on the cord.

Walking once more
the halls   not as a stranger, a visitor –
but a teacher
greeted by faces lighting up
in recognition.

I steal one extra slice
of the years of joy I left behind.
It's not mortality I escape
not the final departure yet...
It's the turning one's head
from the familiar, the comfortable,
the beloved everyday
that's hard.

And so I jumped at the chance
to go back
(like Emily, perhaps, in Our Town)
I too had to go back
to intercoms, to crowded halls,
to tired colleagues, to mammoth efforts
at moving minds forward,
to lessons...those packaged hopes...

I am grateful
this spring morning
(when the earth renews itself
into blossom
and Resurrection seems
more plausible than ever)
and I am once again
"resigned" shall we say –
to gazing into the sun.

Essay Contest: Vashon High School

I sit in the library with signs on the table:
ESSAY CONTEST HELP
I sit waiting for business.

As the morning hours tick by
I draw the curious, the needy, the bored
with their own work –
I deliver my sales pitch
brainstorm various approaches,
offer promises of attention,
and possible fame.

Slowly –
with patience my strongest forging tool –
I welcome reticent foot-dragging, shy girls (mostly)
I welcome the bright ones urged on by their teachers...
all who carry
pages of penciled lines to me.

We sit side by side
read the words
listen for the song and rhythm to materialize
below the surface...
listen for the meaning to assert itself
stand to attention –
glow.

We play with positioning –
move a phrase here, add a phrase there –
we question why this is written
why that isn't....

We tickle the penciled lines until
a bit of passion oozes through
a glimpse of heart
and genuine voice reveals itself.

Then I send them away.

Another day I set out my signs
and – dressed up in my patience
once more – I hope for business.
Now the day is filled with visits
all in assorted stages –
the talking topic stage,
the "walking over the jumbled first words" stage,
the "polishing oil sliding over
typed pages" stage –
(slipping only here and there on verb tenses,
on missing ends of nouns –)

Occasionally a young man shows up
who wants to be part of this "merry-go-round"
of writing drafts.
"Who influences you to be the best you can,
to go on with your education?" I ask.

"Why, I can write about that! I can write about my uncle!"
or another picks his grandmother, or his brother,
or a teacher from 7th grade.

What lovely tributes spill from the hearts
to the pages.
Pages of hope and encouragement light up
the eyes of the young writers
as we move – like a graceful dance –
from draft to draft.

I sit in the library –
my signs now a bit worn but familiar –
a red folder open before me.

The sweet mound of finished products
begins to swell
as the final copies – like gold –
are delivered to me.

But most endearing are the young writers
carrying around their own copies –
like some tender miracle of their own making –
carrying them to teachers to read and be proud,
to have parents read and see
the wonder their child's words can produce.

Ah, the magic, the beauty of the essay contest.

Final Rubric

We teachers
spend our lives
scoring, grading, judging,
evaluating, correcting...
Satchels
full of essays, quizzes,
homework.

We sit in the stands – grading –
at our own children's games
Our hands are never empty.
We spend our evenings,
our Sunday afternoons, scoring,
remarking on hundreds
of student efforts,
or what sometimes seem but shreds
of efforts.

Like judges
at a diving meet
we raise our scorecards
reflecting our call
on a young child's attempts
at quality.

And I sometimes wonder:
how will our dives into the soup
of human experience
be judged in the end?

At that final judgment –
I can hear each of us now:
What grade did I get, Lord?
Will effort count?
Will you show me any mercy
for my effort?
Is there a process grade
along with the final product score?
Do you consider extra credit?
Will the degree of difficulty of my life
be taken into account?
Do you grade on a curve?
What eternal rubric will you be using?
Did I pass?
When I finally do pass...
will it be with honors?

First Day Speech

They file in
nervously looking around
for a familiar face,
for a back row seat.
I stand ready to extend my first dose
of experience –
what they're to expect,

Class:
Here are my rules
Trust me...
trust me to look out for your own good
to know when enough is enough
to challenge you while making sure
you succeed
to be kind and reasonable
(when your life seems to be collapsing
in on you).

Trust me
to do my best to bring the finest
of strategies and experiences
to the material we study.

Trust me
to be fair, not play favorites,
not make you feel embarrassed
unwelcome, but rather
to make you feel safe.

Trust me
to look for the real you under the piercings,
under the makeup, the cool expressions,
strange clothes.

These are my rules.
You will succeed in this course.
It's my job to help you,
trust me.

Foreign Fears

A large hand –
sun and nature browned
calloused and dirt crusted...

Ripped a hole through
the blue summer sky
and reached down
to where I was sitting
on my dock...

And touched me.

This was not God's hand
but rather
the angry touch
of hatred and blind destruction.

For the first time
the actual possibility
of a foreign agenda
pierces my sleepy security
and makes itself visible
here,
where I live.

The air waves
of local talk shows
are full ot it today –
possible Middle Eastern persons
lurking our Our dam
suspiciously close
to the dam's rim
under a blanket of darkness.
Others inquiring about renting boats
asking for information.

What were they doing there?
Just how vulnerable are we?
Could they have picked us
to hurt?
To tear apart?
To vent their unholy anger upon?

The very real hand of fear –
foreign to us usually –
has broken through
and punctured
our membranes
and touched our minds
if not our flesh.

Forever After

If there is a "forever more"
than I know mine...
I imagine everyone walking around
with only a necklace on.

Made of jute or hemp
covered and clustered
with colorful jewels
each holding one
unforgettable experience
in its shiny center.

When we walk up to one another
we reach out and hold
one of the jewels...
reliving that experience
together.

So my dear husband
I can touch that jewel
which holds your favorite
fishing tournament
and reel in those bass
with you once more.

So my son
I can finger that blue sapphire
on your necklace and be transported
to the diving meet
where you first coached a young girl
to a national championship
and taste with you the sweetness
of success.

Or stranger
I can hold a jewel on your necklace
and be racked with the same
unfathomable pain
you felt while watching
loved ones shot down
by distant warlords.

And as we move
from individual to individual
fingering their fright, their fantasies,
their triumphs and failures
(slowly because time has no
power over us now)
we will be brought
to an exquisite understanding
of our collective human condition
and finally
be capable of love.

Fresh Air

A precious commodity –
fresh air...

Today
most of us process
our air –
condition it, cool it, heat it,
clean it, pump it, circulate it –

Today
most windows don't open
stay in position
from one season to the next.

But
I hunger for the taste
of birdsongs floating on breezes
into my bedroom
mornings
with chilled sweet smelling
breezes
slipping through the screens
sliding down my throat.

I thirst
for the sounds of water
and creaking docks –
of herons, frogs
and far off fishing boats...
the single sound
of moon
hitting waves
and bouncing off shore rocks
late at night...

I memorize
these sensuous mornings, midnights
of early spring, early fall
before the tempered need
to close up the house
outweighs
the delicious outside
air.

Frog Songs

They've come
squat little forms
on rocks, in crevices,
floating in my fish pond.

Extended throats
ballooned out into bubbles
fill the air
with extended calls
for mates.

A chorus of high-pitched
trills pierces
the pond's silence.
Sends the fish swimming
in frantic zigzags.

Stately little wads
of dark mottled bodies
with blinking eyes
and a single purpose.

Their songs – a capella –
swim through my night's dreams,
break the daylight,
surge through the noon's sun
and surge their way into evening.

They are simply
relentless –
single minded,
focused.

My little pond
the meeting place for spring's
mating dance.
For spring's call to fertility
in an explosion of sound.

Girl in Black With Raspberry Hair

Smudged eye makeup
black fingertips
big heavy boots and mesh stockings.
Spiky hair
with a spray-painted look
of raspberry and lemon.

Marissa.

Someone's tiny baby once
in pink ribbons
and dainty duck-print dresses.
What baby steps
brought her eventually
to become
the young lady
in my back row
with a chain-like necklace
and mask-like face?

The truth is
she's dazzlingly brilliant
and as the days go by
I begin to see
the jewel of a girl
glow
in wave upon wave
of shimmering color
from the soul up and out
through the black habit
of her choosing –

No.
Marissa can't hide
the miracle of herself
from me –
Not for long.

Good Intentions

Driving south
through Mississippi, Tennessee,
Alabama, Georgia –

We pass monsters
built from kudzu
with telephone poles or dying tree trunks
for bones.

This feral ground cover now molds
and suffocates everything it touches.
Standing like green golems
with leafy pelts
in living green graveyards
while they silently build their own
tombstones and monuments
one foot per day.

I've learned that kudzu
was brought by the Japanese
to this country in 1876.
We enthusiastically nurtured it
to shade southern mansion porches.
Today it covers up to four million acres
in southern states
costing fifty million in farm and forest
production, yearly.

A green idea
dazzling in good green intentions
now rotting in its repercussions.

So true of most school reform plans –
kudzu that smothers and strangles the life
from everything it covers –
A monster of illusive standards,
timeliness,
with no variation or exception,
mindless coverage.
No idea when enough is enough
where individuality loses its attraction
and sameness is the goal –
A monstrous assault
on young lives –
but all done with
the best of intentions.

Gov. Billingham's Mansion
From The Scarlet Letter by Hawthorne

Nothing short
of wondrous –
this magnificent house
with slivers of glass
cemented into the stucco walls
to produce rainbows,
to reflect sunshine,
to mirror back glimpses
of observers
standing dazzled before the door
as did our Hester
and her little Pearl.

Symbols, symbols, symbols...

Hester wades through them
as best she can –
with letter burning breast
with child –
lower case version at best.

Shadows and light,
forests of guilt and loyalty
of love and loneliness –

But that shine-soaked house
blazes in beauty
calling to you both...
here you stand your shaky ground
and claim your pearl of great price
for yourself.

Here within these spangled walls
you fight the words
of witch and demon seed
as never before...

Yes, Hester,
here you grab
your handful of sunshine
for yourself
In spite of them all
in spite of those
hypocrites,
all

Governor Billingham's mirror flecked
house –
revealing to all of us
willing to see –
our personal scarlet letters
our particular sunshine
our moments of satisfactions
of humiliation.

This shingled symbol:
inside a book of symbols
shines through the pages
of Hawthorne's gloomy book
and holds us –
momentarily –
in its spell.

Our Handwriting

The grade school nuns
took handwriting
very seriously –
pages of practiced cursive
measured by rulers
checking for consistency –
bruising our knuckles
with those same rulers
for sloppy R's or skinny O's
or partially crossed T's.

Funny
how some of our rebellion
against strict rules and rulers
came flowing out our pens
through our handwriting –
not in our words
but in our loops and flourishes,
our mix of printing and cursive,
our arches and hearts for dots –
wild experimentation
in those days.

Others' Handwriting

Sometimes
I can look at a loved one's handwriting
and see them whole –
my father's steady and studied
M's and J's and D's
as he signed checks to save me
when money was short.

The scrap of my mother's scribbled
prayer for a cure to her cancer
written on the back
of a recipe card –
now a scrap of writing
so sacred
in her own hand, her own hand.

Black Teachers' Handwriting

I've found
my black inner city teacher friends
have the most beautiful,
ornate, flowing script
as if silently, stubbornly stating:
Here at least I can offer beauty
provide elegance
that should be surrounding
my little charges,
but isn't.

These are teachers
in the midst of the most needy:
hungry for loveliness and orderliness
that is non-existent
in their neighborhoods, their worlds.

These teachers
fill their boards
with lovely letters
that speak of a sweetness
and safety and order.

These teachers use their handwriting
as a magic tool
to heal, to strengthen, to guide...
A tool
providing visible hope
for the future.

These teachers
fight back the blight,
the chaos of an impulsive world
with their chalk, their dry erase markers –
one handwritten word
at a time.

Hemingway's Cats

Everyone takes the tour –
what is a stay at Key West
without a bit of homage
before the old man's Underwood typewriter.

But I wasn't prepared for the cats –
ancestors of Hemingway's lilly, they say –
thy gravestones still mark the names
of deceased favorites – in the backyard.

Was he better, more faithful to his cats
than to his debutante wives?
Were they less demanding?
More accepting of the old man's vices,
self-imposed allusions?

Some cats still have the inherited trait:
six toes on front paws –
strange but there's more conversation
among visitors about the cats than Hemingway.

The human side –
we can relate to a keeper of cats –
far easier than to the master of words
so powerful the American literary world
was set on its ear, so to speak.
Yes, this cat lover was like us –
the writer, though, a man from another place –
a place we know little about...

High Speed Chase

Open the lid...
Push the back key...
Wait for the lights, the jingle,
the Welcome.
Push the icon,
listen to the hum of activity,
then
you're in...

(Our minds need new metaphors
for this sort of space travel)

I jump
from link to link
I dance on a web of
electric silk.
My mind races
while my body – ooh, my poor body –
in a static, trance-like
position
poises lifeless, motionless,
over the screen
for way too long –

I cannot hear my muscles
scream.
If I could,
I'd ignore them anyway.
The pull of color,
the taste of fresh spilled information,
the possible contact

at any moment
with a teeming flowing world
is overwhelmingly
addictive.

Here is a real world
version of Star Trek
beaming me up.
Only here
the mind leaves the body –
The shell of me
remains frozen in place
while I fly into
a strange planet
of megabytes and downloading,
of wizards and rams and preferences
and windows. so many windows.

A precise planet
with passwords for entrance.
A secret world
of webmasters and streaming video –
all contained in a thin box
of grey and silver
with a glowing heartbeat
on its side.

Besides straining my muscles
and hypnotizing my brain –
what has this mechanism
done to me?

Does it need to
feed on my vitality
for its existence?
Has it lead me down a path
of fonts and commands and tools
that I should be wary of
traveling?
Has a virus slipped perhaps,
through the keys
and wormed its way into my head?

Is the robotic age
of the Asimovs and Bradburys and Clarkes
– now masked in my flesh –
virtually here?

High Stakes Tests

I.
Walk into the arena
calm your beating heart
you are ready
you are ready for battle.

Size up the opponent
check its weight, its expanse,
the looks of it –

You've brought your weapons –
the extra pencils
the friendly erasers –
the watch on the desk...
your sharpest weapon –
the brain – is pumped, ready.

Go on, you say –
let me build points
conquer the paper dragon
the ink-marked enemy.

Now skim –
like a tall ship in the sun –
skim the surface of the first piece
pointing out the glimmering
key words, phrases

Notice the setting where this first piece
is couched –
the illustrations, the by-lines,
the tiny print.

Next take note of the enemy's arsenal –
the questions –
prepare yourself for the first attack.
The battle begins
eradicate poor choices one by one –
build graphic organizers
to support your volleys
of well-aimed strikes.

Be razor sharp with your choice of words
back each idea with concrete –
heavy concrete evidence from the text
Never give up –
fight the robot-like standardized
unblinking enemy
until the last one falls
to your pencil.

Don't allow
this heartless pile of inhuman paper
to break your spirit,
smash your dreams,
destroy your future plans.

Fight like the warrior you've become
rack up points
over and over again
rally the strength within you
the taste of victory is close.

II.

Look at us –
creatures bound by standardized ropes
and chains...
How to get that adrenalin pumping
that was first used to beat down
blood thirsty invaders, intruders...
used to conquer the wild
ᵗᵒ ᵐᵃᵗᶜʰ ˡᵉᵃˢᵗ ˢᵗʳᵉⁿᵍᵗʰ ᵃⁿᵈ ᶜᵘⁿⁿⁱⁿᵍ
with the best of the wild creatures –
not for sport, mind you,
ᵇᵘᵗ ᶠᵒʳ ˢᵘʳᵛⁱᵛᵃˡ, ᶠᵒʳ ᵐᵃⁱⁿᵗᵉⁿᵃⁿᶜᵉ.

How to rouse that fever for fight
and glory
when the enemy now
is insidiously quiet
and lying dormant
between test booklet covers.

No shouts or battle cries or songs of war
precede the entry into today's
coliseum –

The enemy is just as deadly
as those of millennium past
lies in wait
and we are numbed before its jaws.

Oh, what a world
we must deal with today.

Hitting a Deer

Not much traffic – 4 a.m. –
just me heading for St. Louis...
Then I see her –
eyes bright with reflected
head lights...
expression (do deer have expressions?)
of surprise
probably reflecting my own
then impact.

I am dazed,
stopped on the highway
realizing I should
move to the shoulder...
dazed and not sure
what happened.

Am I all right?
No windshield crash
no death for me this morning
but where is the deer?

As I get out of the car
shaken
I look back down the road.
A shadowed bulk
sprawls itself
in the right lane.

A second ago
eye to eye
now death to one
and life to another.

Encounters – impact –
most of ours aren't
so dramatic, so final.

Most of us –
meeting eye to eye –
go our separate ways
seldom crashing
into each other's lives
so precisely.
Sometimes the strength
the tragedy
the power on impact
is spread out over
decades.

Ice Storm

Hard to believe
so much danger
held the highways
in cold bondage
yesterday.

Now...
cream clouds and
soft blue skies
with sun...

Unfathomable
sparkle
on ice-coated trees
stuns us
with beauty.

Momentarily...
we forget
yesterday's strain
and discomfort
yesterday's
miserable experience.
Beauty
can do that.

Ideas: Shapely or Flabby?

They need to be played with...
tickled
taken out and exercised.
Ideas need constant
massaging –

If neglected
they silently turn
into pretty little stone
lawn ornaments

Take those easily learned
prejudices...
picked up from family, friends, schools.

If not challenged
by a friendly game
of hand to hand combat, wrestling,
hide and seek, paint ball –
a little rough housing play –
but rather are left to stand in the brain's corner
growing moss on their sides –
they dry
and harden and get too heavy
to move
even if you wanted them to.

Suggestion:
While walking your dog
walk your ideas...
Exercise your thoughts
play with those opinions of yours.
They could use the fresh air
and new spring outfits as well!

Take out those dusty old ideas,
shake them 'til they tingle
with either reaffirmation or doubt!
Keep your mind in condition.

And really
what's sexier
than a shapely mind?
Nothing.

In Memoriam

Between the covers
let me lie in a deep, peaceful sleep.
Let my spirit wait
within my books' covers
for those wishing to visit, to see,
to meet with me
once again.

Let the reading of my words
quicken me to life
and I will thrill once more –
through you –
over the beauty of the moon
rippling over the water...
over the call of herons,
of whip-o-wills at dusk...
over the touch of ordinary
things that accompany us
through our days...

Rouse me from my sleep
when ever you wish,
and I will rise
from between my books' covers
and join you –
walk with you –
once again.

Junk Drawers

They say
poor families don't have
junk drawers –
too transient to develop one.

Junk drawers can't grow
in sterile homes either –
they need time to marinate
their holdings,
to develop roots.

Yes, it takes time
to nourish a junk drawer:
feed it with single items
needing to be paired,
stuff it with bits and pieces
of our lives,
our droppings that can't be discarded
just yet.

Junk drawers
try to take root
anywhere there is a dark space
that can remain undisturbed
for weeks at a time...

Later on
they issue rare fruit –
tiny treasures,
bits of usefulness,
slivers of memory,
items with no other place to go.

(Junk drawers
are orphanages for tiny pieces of life
with no homes
too valuable to discard
yet not valuable enough to earn
themselves a specific place to stay.)

As a child
I loved hunting through
the very public kitchen junk drawer
but even more so
through my father's top dresser drawer –
filled with mysterious objects,
with a fortune in change,
with exotic hints and clues
to what an adult's life
contained.

I wondered even then
what my replica of a drawer
would eventually hold...
when old enough to feed, to tend,
to cultivate my own junk drawer.
A treasure trove it has become, too.
All tiny mirrors of my thoughts,
my desires,

my mundane, concrete values
shoved together –uncatalogued –
waiting silently
in darkness.

The day after my father died
I went through his dresser drawer
one last time.
Lovingly I fingered
the remains
of a life I had loved so well –
still caught up by
the mystery and inlimneness
resting within...

Resting within
my father, of course,
and within
his junk drawer.

Ten Literary Yearbook Notes

Let's say I taught
some of my favorite characters and authors...
what would I write to them in their yearbooks?

Michael Crichton (author)
Mike:
Congratulations on your acceptance into medical school!!
Just one thing – you're still a writer, a storyteller,
don't let that beautiful gift die in
the flurry of Petri dishes and patient charts—

Emily Webb (in Our Town)
Emily:
You are an exceptional student
both of history and daily living –
keep that sense of wonder
over the everyday events in life –
each moment is so precious!
Enjoy them!

Randle P. McMurphy
(in One Flew Over the Cuckoo's Nest)
Mac:
In spite of the trouble maker that you've been all year,
I love your confidence, your instinct for truth,
your unbelievable zest for living!
I'm glad your were in my class.
Good luck!

Edgar Allan Poe (author)
Edgar:
You really have a gift
for making music with your words –
that piece you turned in
for your final assessment –
Bells – was remarkable.
You should try to get it published.
I'll help you if you'd like, keep in touch!

Joyce Carol Oates (author)
Joyce:
Of all my young writers this year,
I feel you have the most drive, talent,
and appetite for writing!
Keep working that theme of cause and effect –
your treatment of it is solid and penetrating.

Truman Capote (author)
Truman:
What a beautiful lyrical style
you are developing!
Have you considered trying
your hand at poetry?
If you do, send some my way.

Pecola Breedlove (in The Bluest Eye)
Pecola, dear, you don't need blue eyes
to be beautiful.
I've seen your beauty –
it shines through you,
through those big brown pools of innocence
and hope you have for eyes.

Huckleberry Finn
(in The Adventures of Huckleberry Finn)
Huck:
You'd be a good student
if your attendance were better.
Enjoy the summer and try
to learn something from your experiences.
See you back in my class next year!

Emily Grierson (in "A Rose for Emily")
Em:
I have a book I want you to read
over the summer: Great Expectations.
There's a character in it, Miss Havesham,
I'd like to discuss with you when you finish.

Stephen King (author)
Stevie:
I know a few of the faculty were concerned
about the gruesomeness in some of the stories
you've been writing for class.
Don't worry... come see me and we'll separate
the "school assignment type" of writing
from the "send it out to publishers" writing.

Luxuries

Three morning hours
to write.
Another hour
to walk.
Two glasses
of good wine
at early evening.

A wood fire
at sunset.
A sighting
of a brilliant red oak
or yellow maple
in fall.

The water temperature
perfect
for lake swimming.
The touch
of my husband's arm
next to me
in the night.

When did my desires
become so clarified?
My needs
so costly?

My life requirements
so intensely
precious?

The Magnificent Leaves of 2004

All conditions were right –
soft, steady rains in spring, in summer
mild temperatures the while
all generating growth
incomparable, unprecedented.

Leaves the size of plates
plump and plenty and forming
so thick a canopy
we saw nothing but green
from our windows
all summer.

And then
brown drifts piled knee high
between house and tiered flower garden –
a parchment-like residue
of summer's growing frenzy.

The conditions were right
and like our leaf bearing trees
luxuriating in unprecedented growth
we, too, have these rare seasons as well.
Rare opportunities
in our careers, our athletic lives,
our emotional worlds,
our intellectual journeys...
when all the stops need to be pulled
as they say –

When such seasons arrive
and are marked with our names
we need to spend ourselves
with such an abandon
that later

if one were to cut across a slice
of our active years
to show the quality and number
of our rings
so to speak –
those seasons of prime possibility
should appear wider,
more pronounced...
provide a deeper stain
than the rest

And with what pride
we would then recognize
each perfect ring
of uninhibited effort

And with fondness say:
Yes, I know those years –
I grabbed them
squeezed the juice from each
until there was nothing left
but beautiful piles
of autumn colored memories
at my feet.

Yes,
I took full advantage
of those right conditions.
I – not just my time –
I am well spent.

Midnight Visitor

In the dead of night
I sit, awake,
as pain, my own private beast,
carves his initials
into my shoulder –
makes my shoulder,
his lair.
I find him
gnawing at my arm –
absent-mindedly
in his sleepy revelry...
while I try to endure.

I have nothing but sympathy
for those whose pain strips them
of their humanness.
There is no nobility to pain
but rather an ignoble grabbing
of breath and wrenching away
of poise and presence...
and yes, at times,
sobs.

I understand now
the urge to take another pill,
try any drug,
listen to any old wives' remedy...
to do anything
to stave off the hot breath
of the beast
as he rummages through my bones,
my tendons, my flesh,
hunting for bits of sustenance.

I don't look forward
to the possibility of my last years –
I'm sure the beast
will remember the tastes of me
and try to return.

Surely those who love me
will help stave him off –
keep him from my flimsy door of flesh,
not let him steal my vanity in his
frenzied gluttony.

Surely
I won't be left alone with him.
Surely,
there will be help.

Mirror, Mirror

We are but glass
at birth
gradually painted
with the quicksilver
of experience.

Our eyes then
become tiny twin mirrors
reflecting back
whole worlds
within, without.

And what if one
peers into our little mirrors
and asks us:
"Mirror, mirror
who is the fairest
of them all?"
What do we answer?

How have we grown
to perceive beauty?
Do we still reflect
only surfaces?
Or have we come to
look deeper
into the pools
around us –
discovering depths
invisible to the naked eye.

Mirror, mirror
just what have we
grown to see?
grown to be?
Tell us.

Missouri Spring

The hickory limbs are candelabras now
with scores of yellow flames ripe for bursting –
perfect tongues of cool flame.

The poor black cherry trees are swathed
in gauzy tents at each juncture – new growth
being consumed by maniacal eating machines
sapping away their life
another sign of spring.

Robert Frost's gold shines across the wooded hills
and stays briefly for those who wait and watch
for its coming.

Migrating finches – three dozen or more –
float like yellow petals from the snowy dogwood
to the ground beneath.
The thistle feeder eager to replenish their energy
on route.

Spring spends her gold magnanimously
in Missouri –
accentuated by red buds and dogwoods –
lacy, wild splendors to thrill the eye
while winding down a rolling,
rural road.

My Son's Tattoo

A cloak clothed mystical
shrouded in darkness
exuding wisdom, power...
All on his upper left arm –
an inked-out remnant
of his sailor days.

But now
he's a highly respected
CPA with a world renowned company
a "suit" some might say –

Yet,
under the "suit" scowls
that other world magician
mocking this current cerebral life
he lives.

Perhaps
all of us should bear tattoos
of our many lives –
have our emotional cries
dug into out flesh –
carry colored ink symbols
of milestones
collected on this journey of ours.

We carry internal tattoos
of course
but there's something
so "on purpose"
about a fleshed out mark –
frozen in needled resolve
we cannot hide or deny
years later.

My Familiars

Little old ladies in nursing homes
have had to let go of most of their things –
the trappings of years of accumulation,
the familiars of years of living.

They have had to choose but a few
to take with them
on the final leg of their journey.

Some have framed pictures
some have little boxes holding
assortments of keepsakes.

As I go about cleaning my house
putting away, dusting, re-arranging
all the tangible items a house is filled with

I wonder how I could melt them down
to a shoe box full
or from my drawers of pictures
select only a couple –
how could I tear myself away
from my familiars – my comfortable things.

But I'm not nursing home material yet
and the soul has not been asked
to wean itself away –
bit by bit from all this earth's stuff
we drag along behind us.

And living has taught me
not to concern myself with possible
problems that have not yet materialized
or fears that only present themselves
in imagination –

So, I buy more drawers to fill,
hunt for still more precious items,
collect pictures of grandchildren
and beautiful trees and sunsets,
and do not worry so much
about where I'll put them later.

Later, when I must travel light
and leave my familiars behind.

Obsession

I gorge on books.

Like an alcoholic
I know where my unread books are
waiting to be read...
I always have a "stash" in reserve.

Like a chocolate lover
my tastes are attuned to a variety of flavors –
heavy reading, light; dark or smooth
or nutty.

Like a binger
I've spent nights awake gobbling down the pages –
staying in bed for whole days
consumed by characters.

Like a gambler
I order good sounding volumes
from blurbs in brochures, in newspapers,
from friend's hunches.
Always taking chances, hoping for jackpots.

Like a collector
I'm vulnerable to come-ons, to bookstores,
to flashy covers and Top Ten Lists.
I double row my bookshelves now.

Like a pro
I play the game--belong to many book clubs –
take the "five for a dime" offers then
cancel after the contract is fulfilled.

Like a lover
I revel in my obsession
see me burning down of the flame
no end to the pleasure
no price too high or costly.

Books. My glorious obsession.

Ode to A House Plant

Indoor plants –
I water, pick off dead leaves, dust...
and usually ignore.
My plants don't get talked to, specially fed,
named, or fussed over.

The slow growing one, though –
a tiny palm tree in two cups of dirt –
has inched its way
into my awareness
after more than twenty-five years
of co-habitation.

I've never considered myself
a green-thumbed lady...
I've never sung to plants to nudge their growth...
But
if plants could whisper back
I'd like to listen.

The tiny palm tree has pushed out
two additional shoots
over the years.
I – I have pushed out four.
Time has seen both of us
mature and age.

Seasonally
I stick Christmas ornaments
in its pot.
Years ago, it held Easter eggs
my little ones hunted for.

I've never replanted it –
same old dirt it originally came in.
Me too, same old skin I came in.

Silent counter of months and moons
observer of life's comedy of errors –
fellow fruit of our ripe old planet...
with affection, I acknowledge you!
I wish you well!

One More Spider Poem

Tiny fishermen
throw their nets out
to the night

Waiting
for flying fish
to catch...
to snag
on the sea of air
that swims through
their sticky nets.

Then at dawn
they collect their catch
repair webs
with gossamer strands
strung from
their little
round-bellied
selves.

Open Letter to Mark Doty (Poet)

I heard you speak on CNN at the Poetry Festival.
My lyrical mind was smitten with you
(if people get "smitten" any more)
I had to meet your words myself, turn your pages myself.

I found your poetry so palpably rich
I needed discipline against swallowing too much at a sitting,
against not allowing proper time for digestion
Like Virgil, you led me into your own Purgatory
at once foreign yet so familiar –
led me in search of your own Alexandria.

Across the Styx of your poetry
I am brought to a land of experience
I have never considered.

You seem unconscious of my presence
yet you respectfully allow me to listen in to your thoughts.
You allow me to step into your mind's rooms and sniff
around the corners
without being chastised for my curiosity.

You are Virgil guiding me into the second story bar
to hear the drag queen's song.
We meet Lola "in a dress with a black tulip sheen"
who blurs my prefab attitudes on gender with a human cry
for wholeness.

You take me to Annie's death bed
and let me hear a whispered promise
to find her, to be there, to calm her dying heart.

Sir, you wield words with the strength of a Samurai,
with the grace of a temple dancer.

Your wise and gentle humanity
breathes a brilliance of truth across the page.
The elegance of your words hushes fears, strips stereotypes,
awakens us.

I had to meet your words myself,
turned your pages...
I have not been disappointed.

Passing the Baton

As a little girl
Jane came to school with me –
helped me stamp books, arrange folders,
prepare for the new school year.

Later
she came to watch the plays,
attend the games,
help me with fundraisers.

Home on college break
she'd sit in on classes,
tell me about her portfolio,
her experiences as a student teacher.

Now all has changed.

Like the runner's baton
the chalk has been passed
so smoothly, so quickly,
that we hardly had time
to notice.

Now I go to her plays,
sit in on her classes,
help her prepare for the school year.

She is the ACTIVE TENSE of education,
I am not.
Hers is the ACTIVE VOICE of teaching
while mine has become
the "try to avoid in your writing"
PASSIVE VOICE

The heady center
of constant motion
and communication
where a teacher abides
is her realm now.

I am but an observer
to the rich, beautiful bedlam
of holding a classroom
together
in cupped hands.

I know this is the way of things,
I'm proud of my daughter,
yet I envy her,
oh, how I envy her.

Pills

Oh my,
all the talk about
costs of medicine –
has become
real.

I am feeling
the squeeze
of purse and pulse
when
told the price
of so-called
discounted
medicines.

I am wondering
if I could
dilute the dosage
to make
the $100-a-bottle
prescription
last longer.

I
am astounded
that
I, the insured,
still need
to shell out
so much
for so tiny
a supply.

(Oh, Canada,
your pharmacies
are looking
more appealing
by the month)

How did we get to this?

America
the land of the
tree...
(Nothing free
about it...)

America
land of the
corporate take over,
the greed driven
price gougers –
the ever-growing
homage
to the bottom line –
success at any
cost.

Where it's not
separation
of church and state
much longer –
but rather
of rich and poor.

America
serving up
a hard pill to swallow
for those of us
sick
of corporation-driven
politics
of aggression.

And
sickened even more
by the renewed
enthusiasm
to ravage the land
and disregard
the environment.

Expensive pills
prescribed by our leaders
despite
the long-lasting
side effects
that might cripple
us all.

Meanwhile,
I trudge to the pharmacy
for another bottle.

Poet to Poet

So
you too?
A word alchemist?
A mixer of magic cocktails
– potent containers –
a player...
A juggler of juxtaposition
a madman.
Yes,
crazy cracker
of symbolic nuts...
a fire cracker
exploding thoughts
into shimmering rainbows – sunbows –

A rhetorical Rambo perhaps
slicing infinites with abandon
crushing connotation
down to a phrase
tackling
a tangle of literary terms
and why?
To get to the guts
of things,
right?

To nudge that AHA!
that means,
"Why, me too!
Yes!
I understand...
you too?
Well said
I've felt that way,
Really
thanks!
Thanks for putting it
into words.
Beautifully
Alive
words."

Positive Feedback

Could we have been
created
for the sheer
purpose
of supplying
positive
feedback?

I know
I look for feedback:
"Fill out this evaluation,
let me know
how things went…"
"Which poem
did you like?"

As the only
creatures
with self-awareness
(as far as we know)
perhaps,
the point
of the whole thing
is really
rather simple:

Perhaps
we're around
because
there needs to be
an audience –
someone
to clap
and be awed.

I can go
with that.

Listen
to our prayers:
"All praise to God...
Give Glory to Him...
Proclaim His
goodness

Aren't these
but
finer forms
of feedback?

Prayer book words
which translated
into the concrete
would sound like:

"Look at that aster!"
"Wow, what a sunset,
good work!"
"What a gorgeous
waterfall, amazing view!"

Are we so
different
from the divine?

Aren't
the same sparks
of desire, of need
mirrored
back
one soul to another
all slivers
of the divine?

Look
for the creator
in that which
has been
created.

And let's
give a little
more
positive feedback
to those
around us –
Why, it's holy stuff.

In fact,
I bet that's
what they call
"grace."

Power Writing

No –
this is nothing
about prescripted
paragraphing –
that
"paint-by-numbers"
essay producing
recipe...

There's no power
in that writing –
only baa-baa-baa
sheep-following
directions
determined to
stamp out
individuality
and produce
a flock
of mediocre
papers
perfectly in step
with each other...
Bah-Humbug!

Power writing –
You know it
if you've ever gotten
stung
by a poem
and watched your
insides
swell up
and had those words
chase you down

and smother you
to the point
of near
suffocation...
That's
power writing
my dear children.

Don't
confuse it
with pablum.

Recognition
– with thanks to James Tate

A pelican landed on the railing of our condo balcony,
"Why, you look like my old aunt Agnes," I said.
"Ridiculous, I'm a bird," it replied.
"No, really, I remember her immensely large
and sagging chin."
"She wasn't a fish catcher, was she?" asked the pelican
steadying himself now on the striped chaise lounge.
I considered the question then responded,
"No, she was an apple pie maker and a good canasta player;
but not a fish catcher."
"Pity," answered the pelican.
"Pity," I agreed.
And sipping my glass of merlot, I felt a wave of sorrow
for myself, my old aunt Agnes,
and a world
of lost opportunities.

The Road Map

The blue veins and red arteries
of Mother Earth –
We touch and cling to them
as we move through life –
drive through life.

Driven by restlessness
moving across plains and down valleys
searching the maps –
mind maps we've each designed

Absorbing the shocks
of wrong turns, u-turns, accidents –
putting miles between today and
yesterday
driven by ambition, desire, goals,
destinations we can almost
touch...

And we note road markers
each birthday inching us further along
and we note billboards
promises of pleasure, comfort, esteem,
resting places to aspire to...

Encased in our travel
we note those moving in tandem
or following or those we follow
for miles.

We see the roadside crosses –
signs of ours and others' mortality –
We see names of towns up ahead
then slow ourselves to catch a glimpse
of how others live,
where others call home.

Hearing the hum of engine and tires
seeing the blur of a wild flowered hem
to the road,
we work to negotiate our place, our speed on the highway...

Occasionally
we consult our map,
check our bearings,
evaluate our progress...

Then, again. set our sights on the sun shimmered horizon,
vaguely aware – aren't we –
that what counts
in the end
what only counts...
is never the destination
but only
the journey.

San Carlos Institute

Cuban freedom fighters
enshrined in niches
and plaster alcoves
raise hands to greet us.

A world of fierce word lovers,
protectors,
exists within these Key West
cream stucco walls.

Many of our times' finest
wielders of pens
have crawled out
from safe,
silent bungalows
onto this stage
of lights, applause,
amplified voices
and hushed attention
to read
what they've written.

To read to
red cushioned seats
filled with would-be writers,
fastidious readers,
aged academics –
those hungry

to be fed by the closeness
of quality, and power, and
confidence –
those hoping to acquire
gifts
that only words can impart.
Most leave
San Carlos Institute
well fed
and amply
gifted.

School Of Fish

I have a different
school to tend to these days –
a school in miniature
without bells, or desks, or books.

Mine is a watery schoolyard
with twenty five charges
all skittish and shy, playful, and
oh, so graceful.

My class of goldfish –
are deceivingly labeled –
since many are not "gold" but rather
orange, black and gold, white,
red and white, all shades –

As were my black students of past years –
not black but honey, ebony,
light brown, pale yellow, bronze,
cinnamon.

(Three of my white fish look like
little girls running around
in their nighties with lacy trim
for fins)

I tend to my school judicially
protecting them
from predators
as best I can

No homework In my school now –
no paperwork, no lunch tickets,
no keeping them in their
seats.

Our days are spent learning
to find cover under lily pads,
burrow into crevices for food,
glide as a group
in synchronized precision.

I diligently assess
their diving, rising, reversing…
how well they use little finned rudders
for control.

A beautiful bunch
whose origins were the local bait shop –
twenty-nine cents apiece –
such a small sum
for so precious a purchase.

There're lots that's precious
about our charges
that only a teacher can see.

My fish –
my gold fish –
my fancy finned beauties
sliding though the reeds –

These little slices of color
against the dark water...
Priceless.

Sequels

It's voice we love, isn't it?
Voice that makes us
buy every new recording,
every follow-up novel,
attend every concert...

It's voice
that supersedes the work itself
and allows us
to forgive flaws, mishaps, stray efforts –

We will always sample
the next sequel...
Hungry for another moment
with that voice
that singular voice.

Second Year's Essay Contest:
Vashon High School

"What is your definition of success and
how can your education help you attain it?"
Tough topic for kids...
Too fuzzy a view of the future for most of them.
So the young people begin to slip and slid over the topic
with no concrete footholds to give them balance
and many,
discouraged with their initial attempts,
give up,
(In fact, avoid me in the hall...decide they're too busy to do
an extra essay...
just can't grapple with the hugeness of the future right now)
Last year
the words slid to the page effortlessly for most –
not this year, not with this topic.

I.
Boy with a Big Vocabulary

A shy smile
an extending handful of pages
"My essay contest entry..."
So I look at the pages of tiny handwritten words...
(Familiar script of a introverted mind filled with worlds alive
and peopled by
quests and journeys and exuberance and swirling whirlpools
of thought)
And I begin the job: edit, sift the wheat from the proverbial
chaff,
the gold from the straw
make the glorious coins of personal thought shine through –
with pen for scalpel I cut, I hone, I polish.
What appears amazes me...
Who is this young thinker walking

the boisterous halls of this inner city school?
How could such phrases bubble up to his consciousness and spill
upon the page?
"I see success as an embossed image on our society
that creates an emphasis in how we envision what we strive to achieve"
Who is this shy young man?

11
Sweet Boy Who Would Have Frightened Me

Another entry...
This time a more concrete idea of success –
I want to be a fireman like my dad –
a sweet essay, nicely structured.
But the writer
tall, a fiercely sullen look, with chiseled features
pushing toward the completion of his adult's man face –
not much child left here –
tattooed arms corn-rowed braids
the body and look of a young black man that would scare us whites
if ever he would walk up to one of us...
And he would wonder at the look of fear he initiated...
He doesn't want to rob or hurt or scare
he wants to be a fireman
he wants to save us.

III.
Girl on a Mission

Her pages come to me ripped from an old planner.
She's angry at what she sees around her –
her own people preying on one another...
"No one wants anyone else to get ahead"
(Her words burn holes in the planner pages with their
passion)
Success is beginning now with tiny steps –
smiling in the halls, being kind to the under classmen –
she will change the world little by little.
A whir young woman all.
taking on her world with the weapons of kindness...
one encounter at a time.

IV.
My Disqualified Dreamer

A strong essay...explaining how she will become a lawyer...
to protect the vulnerable
from the heavy-handed system...
I try to find her to polish, to edit-she seldom shows up –
I ask around, check her records...
Although she's a senior in years, in age,
she has earned only enough credits to place her as a
sophomore...
No graduation for her this spring...
I can't enter her essay.
Is this a dream lovely on paper but existing only there?
So much follow through needed
to pierce the paper and make words walk the pavement
into the real world.

Shad

An ugly name for a graceful fish
skimming over rocks; balancing, sliding
in shallow waters.

Quietly circling velvet green growths
with ten to twenty classmates
in this single school.

Shad are bait fish.
What a job description to carry
on your fins.

These November shad (six to ten in number)
having outlived the summer feeding frenzy
of predators.

Have they outgrown their usefulness
as common feeder fish?
Are they free now to redefine themselves?
By virtue of having escaped fate?

I am awed by their silent weaving patterns at my feet –
inches from me they skim green moss from rocks
and eye me, unconcerned.

Sunlight splashes their silver backs and
gray black underbellies –
perfect fishy shapes swimming
in circles at my feet.

Silently swimming at my feet.

Shortest Day Of The Year

Winter solstice –
visions of pagan rites
of jubilation
of recognition of earth's
revolutions

Not so pagan
really

Those so-called pagans,
Hoolihan
had a strong
mantle
of ritual and reverence
for the cycles of life
we all experience.

And it is in ritual
we remember
to stop, reflect, take stock,
reset our lives' rudders
to point us forward
once more.

Oh, that we were people
whose lives were laced
with a thicker layer
of ritual
as that of our old pagan
brothers.

Today
might find us
setting our internal rhythms
on this solstice
to beat with more
focused intention
and purpose...

With more resolve
to act human

The Starr Interview

The Day of the Interview
Nervous, physically on edge, anticipation loaded
if I only get there on time I'll be fine –
Early – waiting – if only I get started I'll be fine –
don't let them see I bite my fingernails
don't smile too broadly and show my wealth of fillings –

The Interview
Who is this woman babbling away – is that me?
Are they listening?
Am I getting off topic?
What do they really want to hear?
Can I show who I am, what I've done,
what can I do in so short a time?
To strangers?
How was I?
I can't tell at all how I came off...
now I feel I said wonderful things –
but did I?

The Day After
Oh my – how many others were interviewed
– thousands I bet –
all dressed better, more coherent, more calming
in their approaches...
Oh my – I probably made a fool of myself –
they'll never pick me
never.
Or will they?

Three Days Later
I've written all the reasons why it will be better,
easier for me if I'm not chosen
I wrote four lovely rejection letters to myself
telling me how sorry they are they can't pick everyone,
how wonderful my qualifications are
but we're sorry, so sorry.
(How will this poem end? Irony, surprise, melancholy, joy,
how?)

The Announcement
The announcement of my non-acceptance was ushered in
by huge thunder clouds of silence –
No call came –
No sound whatever heralded the loudness of rejection.
The silent phone rang out my regret – no stars in my
clouded sky –
I move my attention out of the vacuum and into
the throbbing energy of tomorrow.
So much for being one of the "unchosen"
I move on.

Thanksgiving Once More

Could this be the last Thanksgiving
we'll spend together?
In a few weeks
the moving vans begin to roll:
one son to Texas
another to Alabama
another in Illinois
and we at the Lake of the Ozarks

A shuttle of the deck of place...
are we aware enough
to catch the threads of relationships
and tie them firmly in knots
so we – a family – won't unravel?

Family rituals
strain, stretch, morph
into different patterns
seemingly without
our conscious choice.

Our hands relax,
the threads slip,
and we awake
with a start
only to wonder what has happened –
why aren't things
as they used to be?

What was it we were thankful for
all those years?

The Beast

Hungry, mad eyes and dripping mouth.
Nothing can satisfy the appetite
of the beast –
nothing satiates pain.
Pain crawls into your awareness
and suddenly there it is –
throbbing wave upon wave
of electric jolts
eating away at one's ability to focus
chewing down to a handful
the bones of usefulness and normalcy.

It crawls into the night...
Night: what was once the deep,
velvety cushioned retreat
is now but the appointment.
The long quiet immersion
that can not be run from, escaped,
avoided.
The beast will not negotiate,
will not listen to logic,
to excuses, to pitiful begging.

Who ever described pain
as a burning away of impurities
a path to a finer self,
a chastened and improved being,
was a fool.

Pain leaves you
a groveling, unfocused weakling
with thoughts solely caught up
in a single cry for relief.
A gibbering hunt for numbness –
there is nothing of beauty in pain.

The Brain

No manual is attached
when the stork delivers the brain
wrapped up in baby flesh.
We have to go it alone,
figure out how it works by ourselves.

Ironically
it seems to thrive
on variety, novelty, surprise
while needing routine as well
for optimum flow.

We find ourselves
picking our brain
then storming it
trying to shake loose the magic
from this heady home
of our personality.

We know so little
about how we know, what we could know.
Know*now*knowledge*
(Oh, look at the NOW tucked
so gently inside all knowledge!)

Awareness always
at WAR with what has been
or might be tomorrow.
(Oh, look at WAR stuck
so tightly inside awareness!)

I like to think –
think that we tease the brain
into unfolding its secrets –
tease by gently pulling at a thread

of thought
until it unravels a bit...
allows that thread
to be spun loosely with other threads
until a shimmering fabric
of possibility
eventually forms a pattern
producing an IDEA.

Or perhaps
forming a QUESTION
that reorders what seemed the way of things –
pressing us to rearrange, readjust
the mechanism of SIGHT
to hold a new view, an INSIGHT –

These are the buds of the brain
that unfold the map we follow,
that pour out so many a tangled mix
of metaphors constantly in need of
sifting, sorting, arranging –

So the thought thread
leads to the fabric
then to the pattern
to make room for buds and maps
as well.
And all the while not tying us up too tightly
in a web of words –
but rather clarifying, clarifying.

Oh, the magic mechanism of the brain.

The Cause

I think
we did save the whales,
didn't we?
We saved the eagles,
the wolves,
the spotted owls...

Now we need
to save the readers!
They're dwindling down –
their habitats are being polluted,
destroyed –

Take airports...
always a rich breeding ground
for the mature reader –
role model for the young –
now filled
with televisions,
people's phones playing
video games,
computers running movies...
All distractions,
excuses,
not to read.

And the I POD…
with audio books,
i-tunes
by the thousands
in the hands
of those
sunning themselves
at beaches and pools
instead of reading
paperbacks.

Danger –
danger of extinction
is on the horizon –
Let's take up a
collection
start a rally
pass a bill
buy a bumper sticker.

Save the reader!
Save the thinker's culture!
Act fast
before it's too late!

Haircut

Revision is nothing more
than a good hair cut.

The substance stays intact
the extra weight –
thinned out.

And we are word beauticians
lovingly washing out the old phrases
trimming the excesses –
adding more bounce, sheen,
conditioning the diction.
Applying highlights
to accentuate the original shade
to brighten the context...
We cut the edges
shape and style to flatter
the look, the feel –
a precision cut.

We mimic a model
from a glamour magazine
or follow the customer's directions...
then

Add a spray of concrete verbs
for a better hold...

Revision –
a poem's haircut.

The Inservice Workshop

Coffee mugs, polo shirts in school colors with logos on the
pockets,
teacher sweatshirts, denim dresses, apple appliqués
(you can tell us a mile away)
Comfortable shoes, notebooks ready for use,
open faces ready to learn...

But more is only to collect ideas we can use tomorrow in class
—
(secretly really hoping for that perfect handout
that will keep the bad boys quiet, spark the smart ones
to do that perfect project...make us feel
we're making a difference...
make them – and us – love our teaching!!!)

Do we expect too much?
No! I'm ready (you should say) Come on – give me jewels
to bring back to class tomorrow!!

Give me back my hope and enthusiasm I started with years
ago –
help me remember why I'm a teacher
help me kill the numbness of the everyday routine
and feel again.

Help me take a risk, throw away the purple years' old dittoes
help me be the teacher
I know I really am!!!

The Mystery of Keys

Key West
named appropriately
since I was handed
three keys to get into
my one bedroom condo –

A key to open
the electric gate to the garage
a key from the garage
to the lobby, the elevator,
a key to two of the three
locks on the door
of the condo itself...
How safe I feel
here at the Keys!

The irony, though,
rests in what I learned
quite by accident:

Not paying attention –
thinking of fish and sail boats and sun block –
I stuck my key into my neighbor's door
and it opened.

Like Alice amazed
at landing in Wonderland
or Dorothy in Oz
I rushed
without thinking into the doorway
and was struck by the fact
that the red onion on the counter
wasn't mine –
the brown shoes by the wall
weren't mine –

I left – heart pounding –
so much for the
safety of keys...
the silly safety of keys!

Now
through the many mirrored reflections
offered by my condo,
I catch a glimpse each morning
of the red onion/brown shock
neighbor on his balcony.
This morning he's only wearing
a towel after

So much for the safety
of keys.

The Passing

We can only speculate
but isn't it
more difficult to be
the one left
than the one leaving?

Letting go
and allowing oneself
to sink down
into the quiet feathered place
of peace
without fear
without pain
without the multitude
of worries
that flutter like moths
within the brain...

Surely
this untightening
of the hands' grip
on the life threads
is easier
than
the condition
of those who
remain...

Those who stand
Helpless – by the bed –
emptied
by this event
so unlike any that's come before...

Who stand
Gutted - washed clean –
by the wave upon wave
of utter sadness
that rocks the body
and floods the mind
with unutterable
darkness.

And where in the light?

Is it only the one
moving on that took
the light?

Is there none left
for those of us who remain?

How are we meant to stumble on
without some light
to guide our steps
once again?

Feeble at best
the future path appears
where we – the ones left –
must begin again
to travel.

To learn anew
how to walk alone –
so foreign a path,
so strange a path.

There is a resilience
though
to our species.

There is a deep-seated joy
in one's very existence
that is part
of our very core.

That inner flame –
but an ember of a flame now –
will brighten eventually
as time soothes us.
As we grow more familiar
with this new and
uncomfortable journey.

Like a child –
learning to crawl, then to walk –
we begin again
to piece together ourselves, our days,
and go through the motions
until the meaning of it all
returns.
And we – the walking wounded –
are once again
of value to others,
to ourselves.

The Pen, The Ink

Magic slides from the tiny point
and slips upon the page.
How – in the scheme of things –
would anyone have guessed...

The wonder of words –
tiny containers of thought –
flowing out of this tube upon the page.

We have evolved, I'd say –
we, the flower of a planet's living growth –
now able to speak not in tongues perhaps
but in pens.
Speak through pens...squeeze our heart's longings
through pens to page.

As huge as the universe we float in is,
so tiny is the miracle of pen to paper;
and yet the unleashing of a universe of thought
flashes light more explosive than any starshine...

In the silence of our rooms,
attending to pen,
inking out our mind's internal journey...

We flash our soul's voice
across generations and centuries...
We challenge the speed of light
with the page that might be opened at any moment.

Here is true time travel!
the meeting of minds generations apart...
The voices flowing through pen and ink
into the future; from far in the past.

The tiny time machine – my pen –
sends my purest essence out to the world
for ages and ages.

The Poet

And so
I am writing off
into the sunset
on a black pen named
Vision.

I write along
with an urgency,
leaving clouds of dust
and a paper trail
a mile wide

For anyone
brave enough
to follow.

The Poetry Reading

A tiny library room
so crowded with chairs
we need to step over each other
to reach an empty one.

The slight figure
in the front
has already begun reading...
seemingly oblivious
to the shuffle of feet
and scratch
of repositioned chairs...

Soon we begin to notice
the man's words
appearing to plump up, bloom,
and like so many iridescent soap bubbles
float over our heads
only to explode
and drip onto our hair, our shoulders...

The bubbles stop
as the man turns the page
for another reading.

Then we notice a molten lava flow
from the top of his head
beginning to ooze up and catch
each word on fire
as he reads...

The fire
starts sucking the air from the room
and although we find it hard
to breathe
we are too caught up in the spectacle
to complain.

In fact,
we dare not move
lest we too would burst into burning
as his lines and stanzas
now glow and blacken with heat.
Just at the point
we think we must surrender
to our own destruction
or run –
the lava cools.

The heavy air expels itself
from the room –
slides under the closed door
and disappears.

A welcomed breeze
of unblistered words
begins to spray a fine mist
over us –
and we sigh.

Abruptly,
the session comes to a close
and we, wet with words,
blink
and shake the remnants
of the reading
from our clothes...
check our program

for where we should be headed
next.

The man at the front –
Spent –
retreats back into himself,
gathers his papers up
to leave.

And each of us
silently questions ourselves:
did we indeed experience what
we thought we did?
Were the words as real as
we had imagined?
How lucky are we to have survived...
unscathed...
Or did we?

The Sermon

Inside the wooden lid of the red desk
lie scraps and scribbles
of student voices.

One in particular
re-awakens a flood of moments
unforgettable for all
present in class that day

We were giving our sermons –
oral mimics of Jonathan Edwards' –
each in a tirade of oratory frenzy –
attempting to change behavior
found to be reprehensible.

Matt takes to the podium.
We listen as he addresses
our inclinations toward prejudice
that need correcting.

We all nod in agreement.
Then he verbally nudges us
toward his specific focus.

With laser clarity and light
our orator directs our attention
to homophobia.

Now, I always urge my young speakers
to put flesh upon abstraction,
build bones within generalities...
and so he does.

With an iron discipline of voice and tone
our orator opens his own personal
Pandora's box.
And with a voice of simple resignation
and raw vulnerability,
he tells his story of dawning awareness,
fright, then eventual acceptance
of an understanding far beyond
what most of us are ever forced to confront.

My young speaker
explains to us that he is gay.

My class is frozen in place.
Wrapped in the exposed tone of the moment
no one moves, few breathe.
And on our fellow student moves
into a plea for acceptance, understanding.

The bell rings –
in those seconds stilled
now in the amber of memory,
I realize no one moves –
no shuffling of books, of papers,
of bookbags – nothing.

In respect
my students allow their fellow classmate
to continue.
To finish in dignity
the sermon that will invisibly define
the year for him,
for his companions.

And I?
I am grateful my room
could provide so safe a haven
for such sharing.

And gently I close the red desk's lid
upon the rough draft of a life
that will not be easy.
But a life that has touched us
awakened in us our empathy, our unity,
for even so brief a moment.

The Squirrel Hunt

Four squirrels
stripped and readied
for the crockpot –
now baggied up
in the freezer.

An autumn morning's hunt.

I'm afraid that the slow changes
in hunters from years ago
to recreational hunters of today
can be found here
in my freezer.

Today's new line of hunters
have no squirrels dressed out –
have no patience for tiny game
but rather mark calendars
for the bigger seasons – turkey, deer.

But it's when one hunts squirrels
in early October
that a man prepares for the big hunts.
Reacquaints himself with his woods,
fills himself with the need for quiet,
and the early hunters' heightened
awareness
of change, movement, markings.
The soul of a true hunter
isn't always draped in expensive gear
and fancy catalog trappings.

It's recognized rather by its devotion
for reunion with the earth,
for reawakening the challenge
of drawing out the wild –
into the open, into range.

The hunter joins himself, thus,
with all who have come before
and succeeded
in bringing home sustenance –
Game.

It's through a squirrel hunt
that the young are taught
the skills of this age-old ritual.
Here is when the young
are introduced to their first
experience of life then death,
of life then food,
of the oldest of all living cycles.
Here is were reverence
for the kill is born –
if it is to be born.

It's the squirrel hunt
that brings out the teacher
in a man,
and the wide-eyed learner
in a boy.

Truth Serum

A discovery
over the years
of jotting down verse
after verse.

"If the truth be told…"
it's always told
drenched in ink
and dried into a
permanence of poem.

I've discovered
the medium makes
for more demands
than clever word choice
or tight metaphor
or lilting alliterative language.

I've discovered
the medium demands
an emboldened truth
that leaves no room
for frilly excuse
or finger pointing accusations.

No.
It yanks the truth
from years of justification
and fabrication.

Naked emotions
are toweled dry now
by sheets of words.

New eyes
are forced to stare
and reevaluate
old lines, old
self-fashioned sound bytes
of memory
of excuses...

What power poem making
exerts on the maker.
I can't muster
the strength to lie
to change the situations
to air-brush the realities
to hide a burnt fillet of facts
Under layers of literary gravy.

Can't do it –
not here.

Twenty-Three Diamonds in the Oak Tree

Deep winter –
frozen world this early dark morning.
Sky diamonds cluster
around, among, upon, between
black leafless limbs
of the tallest oak

Organic lights
these few days before
Christmas.

Yes,
I have a real tree
with real lights
with a spangly spectacle
only early risers
enjoy.

The template
Christmas
tree.

Visiting My Children's Homes

It's early morning –
I'm writing
in my youngest son's kitchen.
Outside a wedge of geese
cuts across the sky,
across the Alabama pines
bordering his property.

My son and his new bride's home.
I am the guest
for whom they lay out towels,
see to my needs –
both real and imagined.

And so it's been –
another son in Texas,
a daughter in Missouri,
my eldest in Illinois.
I've been a guest.

Secretly –
as all the pleasantries
are attended to,
and the goings on of life
accounted for...
when all the tours of towns
taken –

Secretly
my heart races
as my mind crowds itself
with a time just yesterday
when these adults
were under my care –
clinging to my knees for cookies
and pleas to be picked up.

Wasn't it just yesterday?

And I was the center
of their tiny universes then
and I chose their clothes,
their playthings, their house.

We raise them for this
independence, self-sufficiency –
but when it comes
and we are the guests, the company,
observers now
of our children's lives and efforts
to tend gardens
juggle jobs and mortgages and such –

When it actually comes
something deep inside cries out,
longs for those yesterdays...
But we catch ourselves
and gracefully tuck away
those thoughts
and ask to help with the dishes.
We are grateful
to be their guests –
we are.

Warning to Young Writers

It's possible
to drown in a sea of words –
choke on words
get them caught
in your windpipe –
stuck inside.

You can
say too much, write too much
and wish
you had more discipline
to yourself.

It's possible
to lose sight of the shoreline –
what with all
the waves of words
slapping against your face
clouding your vision
crowding your mind
with overflow.

And when you
lose sight –
the torrents of wet words
simply
run down your back
float away
in rivulets
while leaving you
dry to the bone
inside.

Beware of the flood
that drowns
and leaves you
thirsting
for a pure sip
of clear thought, of insight.
Better to dry the salt tears
and re train the pen
to be wary
of excess.

What Happened...

To the early teen who watched
horrified
as her hips expanded, her waist disappeared,
her body turned suddenly
into a version of her mother's?

To the sophomore
who fell hopelessly in love
with the girl who sat in front of him
in biology –
who wasn't the same color as he?

To the senior
who had breezed through these
past twelve years
on his smile, his personality –
first at everything, best at anything
yet couldn't really read?

To the sweet little girl in the first row
who played school during the summer
and loved her perfect papers,
penmanship, punctuation –
who wanted to be the perfect teacher?

To the bully who thrilled
at bringing others to tears,
who thrived on dishing out
humiliation year in and year out?

To the silent kid in the back row
who watched everything with glittering eyes
yet never volunteered a word?

To the young man
who cheated on every test,
copied every assignment,
forged every note or pass
but never got caught?

We who remain
would like to know –
would hope the inevitable
didn't happen...
would like to be surprised.

While Teaching Morrison's
THE BLUEST EYE

Last night
I dreamed of a large brown woman
draped in yards and yards of warm umber material.
She held above her head
a steaming wooden bowl.

Gathered around her feet
(with heads bowed and bared)
were my students – kneeling in anticipation.

Without warning, yet expected,
boiling black ink – liquid words –
spilled down upon their heads in a burning baptism.

Will they be all right?
Will understanding be the glaze when pain cools?
Will the residue be compassion?

With new eyes the world seems older...
and an innocence – inked out.

White Page

Before the emptiness
I stare, I poise the pen
I wait...

So many people
walking the planet
with poems that never get
pealed from the brain
slapped upon the page...

Habitual authors
with books up their sleeves
never to dribble
down to paper...

It takes
a mix of elements
to let the word kites fly
from the brain:

Courage –
yes, above all, courage –
Humility –
(as the fearsome blank page
shines forth)
that given the chance

whole worlds will appear
soon in print
from nothing –
Patience –
one can't force this magic –
Opportunity –
yes, one must present a time
and place familiar to the

secret muse
that nudges the thoughts
to bubble up
on command.

A fearsome venture, this,
not unlike
dragon killing as a career.
Sometimes
nothing of value appears
sometimes it does.

We humans have so little understanding
or control
over the magic we possess...
to turn white pages –
as Rumplestilskin changed straw –
into gold...
lovely worded gold.

Why Books Will Endure

We like the weight
the feel, the texture of the pages.
We like
the rhythmic ritual
of page turning.

We like
to hold a ... book read
against our chests
our minds filled with characters.

Nothing –
the audio-tapes, computer scrolling lines,
iPods full of words –
nothing will satisfy the heart
of a reader
quite like the physical companionship
of a book in hand.

And afterwards
when the time spent holding words
in both hands
is over
we place this book
reverently
on one of our many shelves
like a good friend's photo
to look at later
with fondness...

Wind Chill Factor

Now I know
how cold
I am...

Until
I turned on
the news
I just guessed –

Now I know

As a kid –
was I warmer
before
they blessed us
with the knowledge
of the wind chill factor?
Before I knew?

And did people
consider themselves
less poor, perhaps,
until
they heard what income
designates
a state of poverty?

What of the person
who felt smart
and capable
until
he was told his
I.Q...?

All hail
facts...
Yes, of course...

But...
weren't we
warmer
before we knew?
Richer
before we heard?
More intelligent
before we were told
the truth?

The truth might
set some free
but it also might
set our teeth to
chattering –
our stomachs
to growling –
and
our minds
to doubt.

The Word Gatherers

At dawn
methodically collecting words
for the day's morning pages,
the day's poem.

Methodically collecting words -
sampling sound, choosing precise shades for
the day's poem -
fitting the now ripe thoughts together.

Sampling sounds, choosing precise shades,
plucking fresh verbs for new metaphors,
Fitting the now ripe thoughts together,
avoiding hardened clichés.

Plucking fresh verbs for new metaphors
lovingly clustering alliterations into baskets
avoiding hardened clichés
with words heavily weighted with connotation.

Lovingly clustering alliterations into baskets
choosing words alive with terrible screams
with heavily weighted connotation –
outbursts of human emotion.

Choosing words alive with terrible screams,
we arrange them quietly upon the page.
Outbursts of human emotion,
we logically arrange – in silence –upon the page.

We are the word gatherers.

About the Author

Mary Kim Schreck, a life-long educator in Missouri public schools, currently is serving as an independent educational consultant across the state. She lives with her husband, Bernard, at the Lake of the Ozarks. Her first book of poetry, PULSE OF THE SEASONS, was published in 2004 by Tigress Press, LLC.

A Note from the Author

Dear Reader:

If perhaps you find that one or more of my poems resonate with your own experience, I would appreciate your telling me which ones. Email me at marykim@aol.com with their titles. MKS

Pulse of the Seasons

By Mary Kim Schreck

PULSE OF THE SEASONS is a contemporary look at life through the eyes of Missouri poet Mary Kim Schreck. Lyrical phrases rich with experience interact with the concrete words of day-to day living as Schreck skillfully weaves poetry everyone can read and relate to. From a fanciful take on how birds might view bird feeders to a beautiful poem on the black women who are the "Women Who Raise Other People's Children," she creates settings that transport her readers into detailed settings they might never see otherwise. This collection of verse is a journey worth taking.

ISBN 0-9761315-0-1 $8.95 US

*   *   *

Tigress Press LLC
P O Box 30859
Columbia, MO 65205-3859

Please add $2.00 for shipping and handling for the first book and $0.75 for each additional book. No cash, stamps, or COD's. Prices and availability subject to change. Payment must accompany all orders.

NAME_____
ADDRESS _____
CITY _____ ST_____ ZIP_____
EMAIL _____

I have enclosed $_____ in payment.
ORDER VIA CREDIT CARD at:
www.tigresspress.com/books/index_pulse.asp
CHECK OUT OUR WEBSITE: www.tigresspress.com

The Red Desk

By Mary Kim Schreck

THE RED DESK is another of Mary Kim Schreck's lyrical masterpieces. With a theme slanted at education, Schreck takes a hard look at essay writing, then slips off to describe a school of fish. From the title poem **The Red Desk** on the first page, this consummate poet delves into things both educational and mundane, and she writes with such compassion and comprehension that the reader is swept along on a magic carpet ride of words. Even if you've never read poetry before, take time to view life through Schreck's eyes. It'll wake you up to all kinds of new perspectives.

ISBN 0-9771601-0-6 $9.95 US

* * *

Tigress Press LLC
P O Box 30859
Columbia, MO 65205-3859

Please add $2.00 for shipping and handling for the first book and $0.75 for each additional book. No cash, stamps, or COD's. Prices and availability subject to change. Payment must accompany all orders.

NAME_____
ADDRESS _____
CITY _____ ST_____ ZIP_____
EMAIL _____

I have enclosed $_____ in payment.
ORDER VIA CREDIT CARD at:
www.tigresspress.com/books/index_reddesk.asp
CHECK OUT OUR WEBSITE: www.tigresspress.com

Printed in the United States
131510LV00005B/19-21/A